PREFACE

Classical music lovers have valued this famous volume of piano literature since it was first published at the beginning of the twentieth century. It was (and probably still is) the largest collection of piano music available in a single volume—covering "all the important fields of musical composition, including classical, modern, light, sacred, and operatic selections." Authoritative and comprehensive, this book soon became the most popular piano collection of its time.

Over the decades, *Masterpieces of Piano Music* has brought pleasure to countless pianists, teachers, and students—and it has earned a treasured place in thousands of college and home libraries. It is to be hoped that this present edition will continue to fulfill the role of the original volume—"a universal piano collection" that provides its owner with "all the standard compositions one would care to permanently possess."

Each of the selections in this restored edition have been newly edited and engraved to allow the contemporary pianist to enjoy anew these gems of the standard piano repertoire.

CLASSIFIED INDEX

CLASSICAL COMPOSITIONS

MODERN COMPOSITIONS

MASTERPIECES
OF
PIANO MUSIC

*The most popular collection
of classical piano music ever published.
This authoritative volume contains
over 140 selections—covering all fields of
classic, romantic, modern, light,
sacred, and operatic music.*

Selected and Edited by
ALBERT E. WIER

Amsco Publications
New York/London/Paris/Sydney/Copenhagen/Madrid

Selected and Edited by Albert E. Wier
Project Editor: Amy Appleby

Order No. AM 967505
US International Standard Book Number: 0.8256.1830.4
UK International Standard Book Number: 0.7119.8506.5

Exclusive Distributors:
Music Sales Corporation
257 Park Avenue South, New York, NY 10010 USA
Music Sales Limited
8/9 Frith Street, London W1D 3JB England
Music Sales Pty. Limited
120 Rothschild Street, Rosebery, Sydney, NSW 2018, Australia

Printed in the United States of America by
Vicks Lithograph and Printing Corporation

LIGHT COMPOSITIONS

SACRED COMPOSITIONS

OPERATIC COMPOSITIONS

ALPHABETICAL INDEX

LOURE

Johann Sebastian Bach

Allegro moderato

PRELUDE IN C
(from *The Well-Tempered Clavier*)

Johann Sebastian Bach

BOURÉE

(from the *Second Violin Sonata*)

Johann Sebastian Bach

MINUET IN A

Luigi Boccherini

RONDO ESPRESSIVO

Carl Philipp Emanuel Bach

CAPRICE

(from *Alceste*)

Christoph Willibald von Gluck

Andante

p grazioso

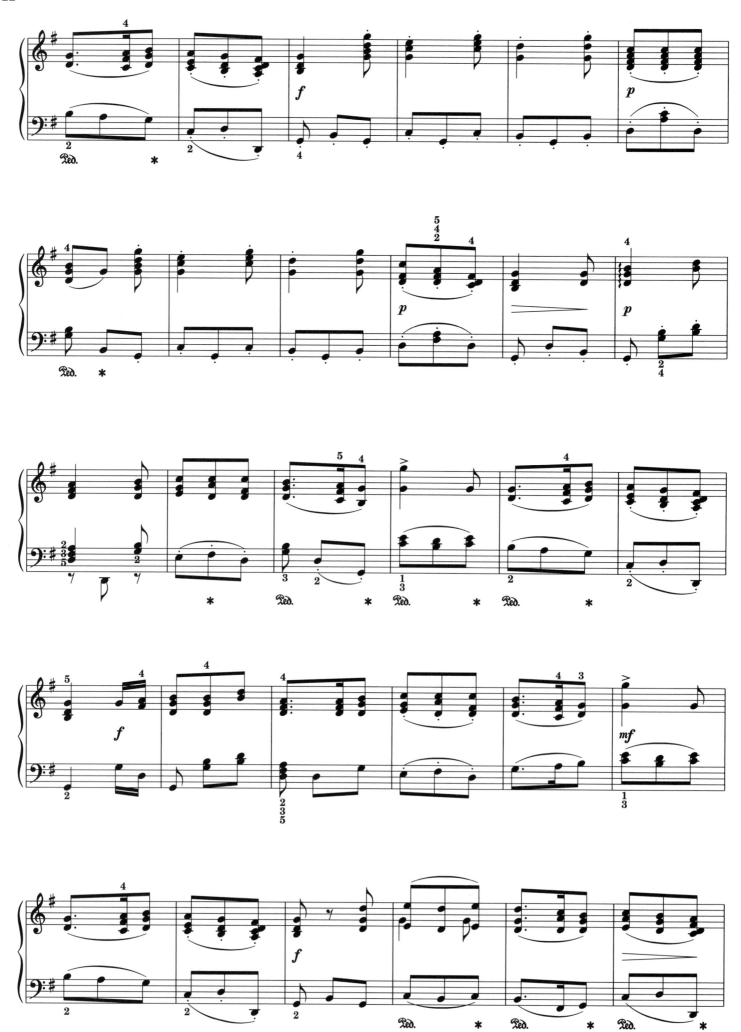

GAVOTTE

François Joseph Gossec

BOURÉE

George Frideric Handel

ANDANTE
(from *Orfeo*)

Christoph Willibald von Gluck

SARABANDE

George Frideric Handel

LA TAMBOURIN

Jean-Philippe Rameau

ALLA TURCA
(Turkish March)

Wolfgang Amadeus Mozart

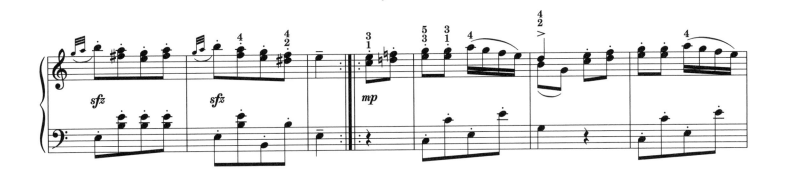

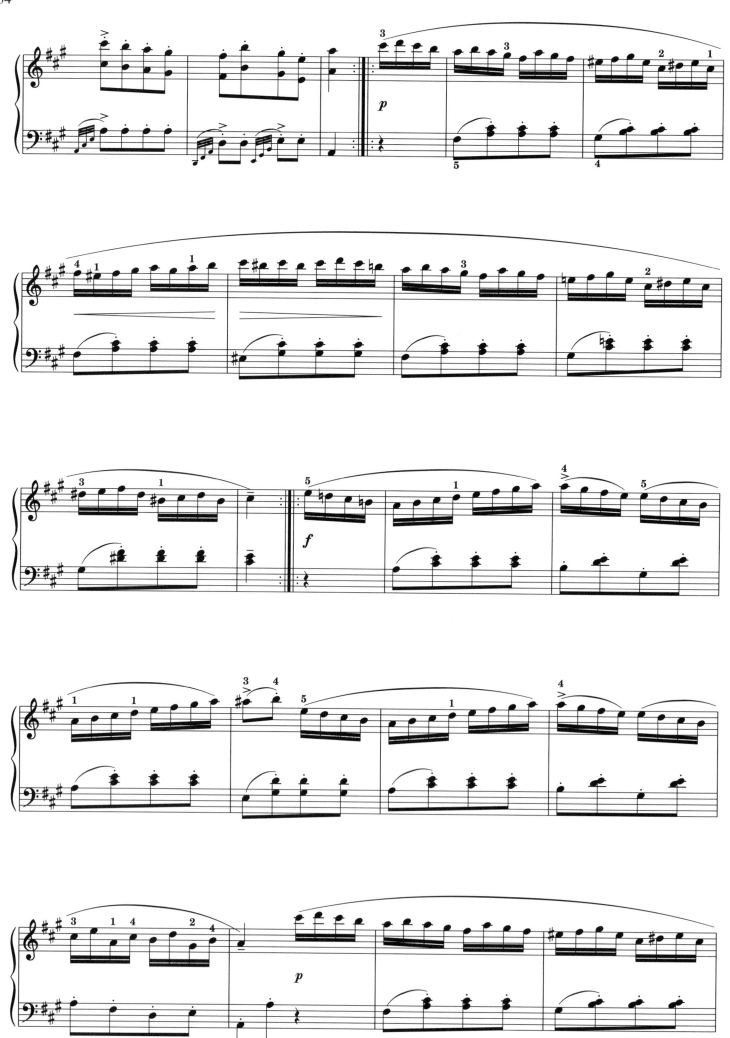

GYPSY RONDO

Franz Joseph Haydn

Maggiore

GAVOTTE

Jean-Baptiste Lully

Allegro non troppo

46

Musette

Fine

sempre legato

D.C. al Fine

MINUET

(from *Divertimento No. 1*)

Wolfgang Amadeus Mozart

SERENADE

Franz Joseph Haydn

TEMPO DI BALLO

Domenico Scarlatti

MOONLIGHT SONATA

Ludwig van Beethoven

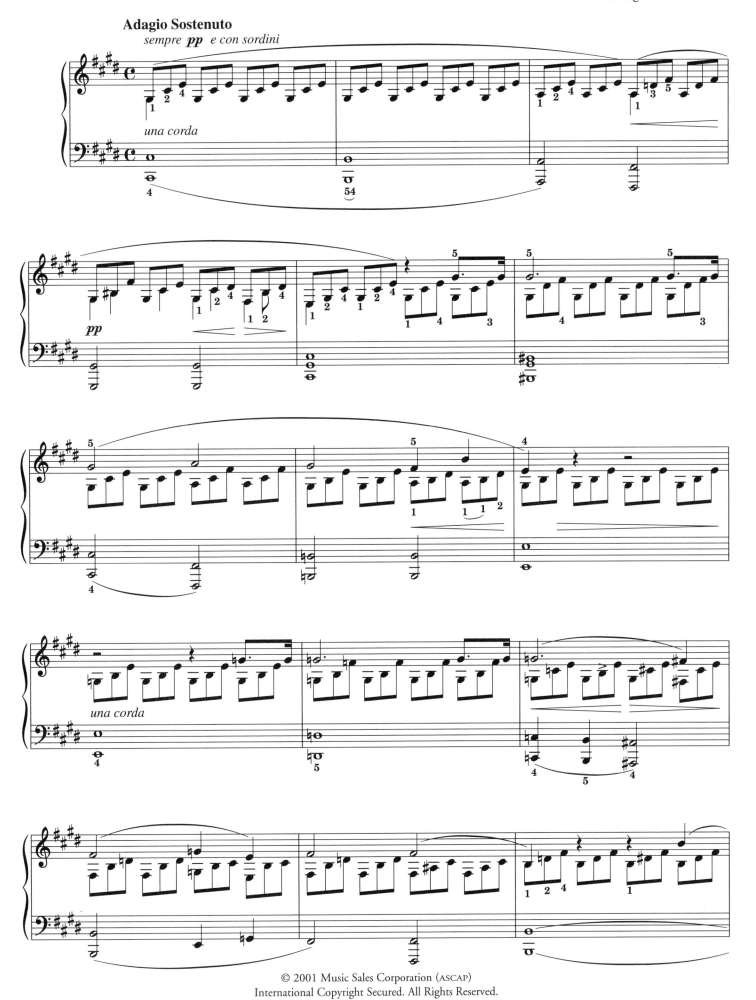

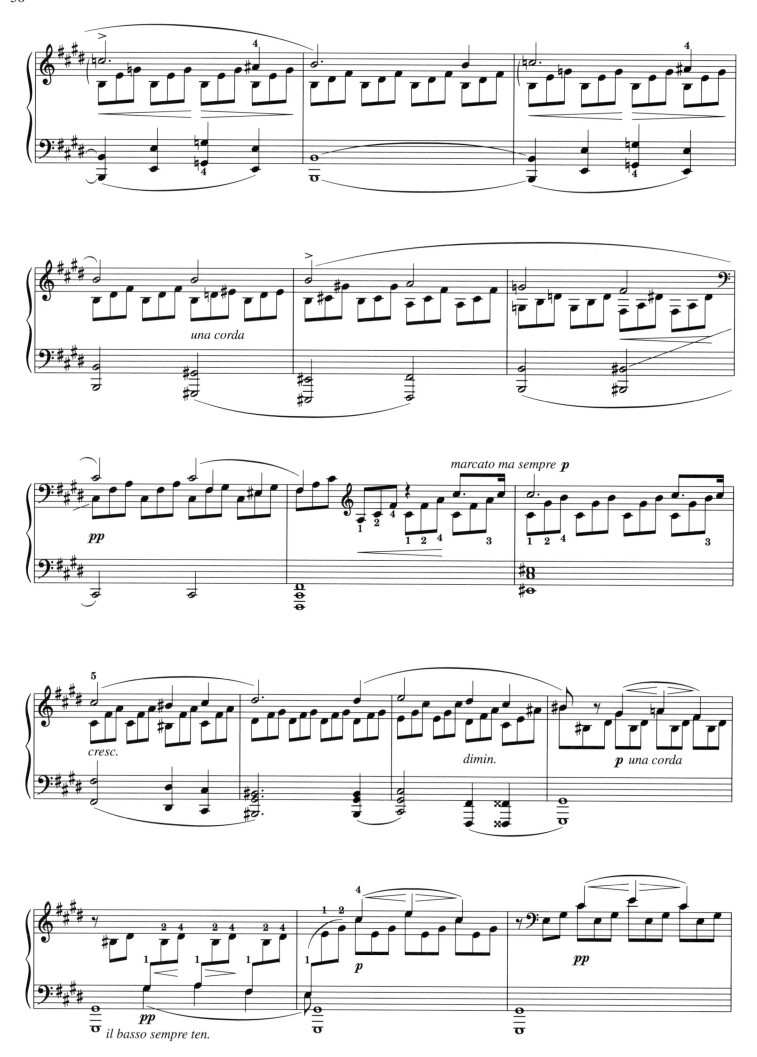

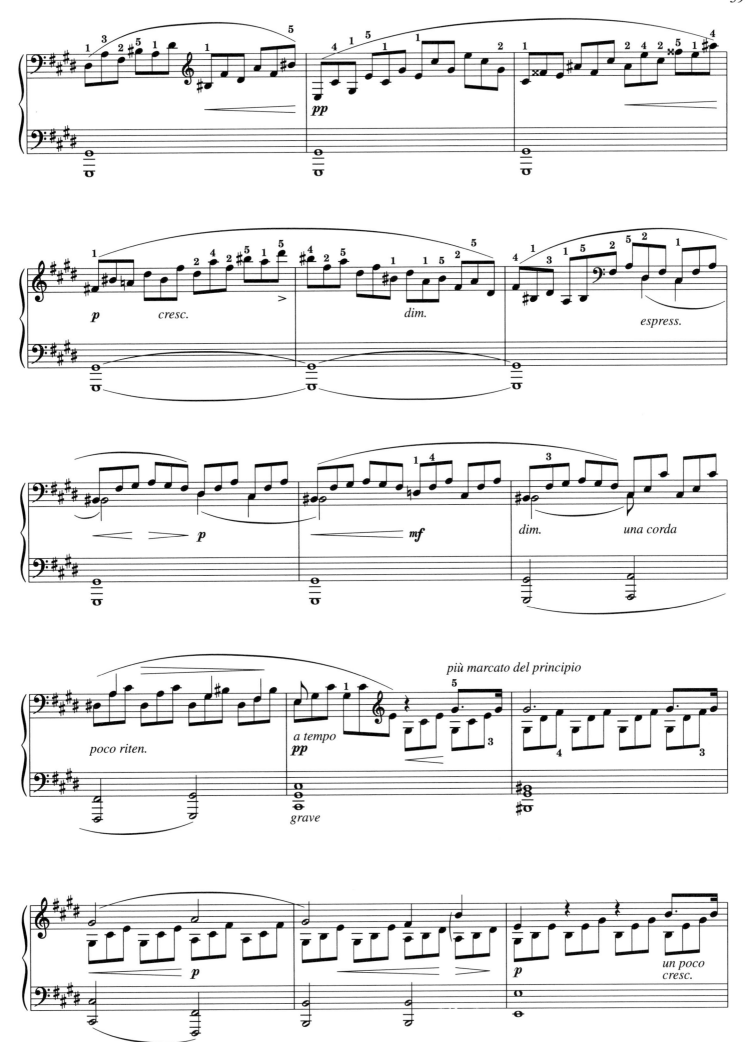

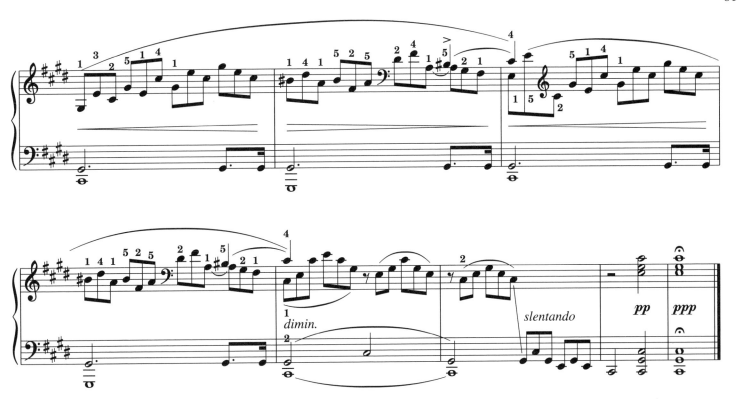

WEBER'S LAST THOUGHT
(Dernière Pensée Musicale)

Carl Maria von Weber

FÜR ELISE

Ludwig van Beethoven

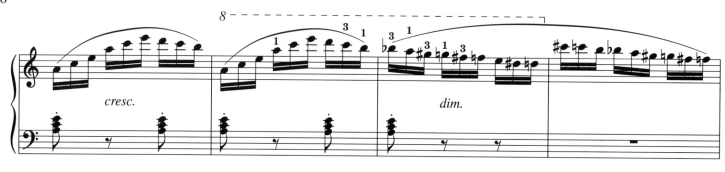

AN ALEXIS

Johann Nepomuk Hummel

MINUET IN G

Ludwig van Beethoven

Tempo di minuet

MOMENT MUSICALE

Franz Schubert

Allegro moderato

UNFINISHED SYMPHONY

Franz Schubert

Moderato

MARCHE MILITAIRE

Franz Schubert

D.C. al Fine

SERENADE

Franz Schubert

NOCTURNE

John Field

Cantabile, assai lento

MINUTE WALTZ
(Op. 64)

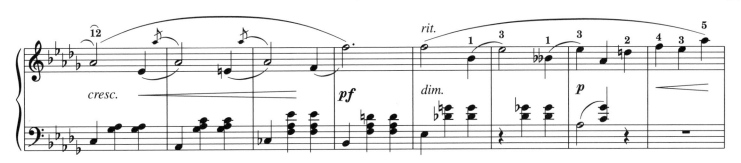

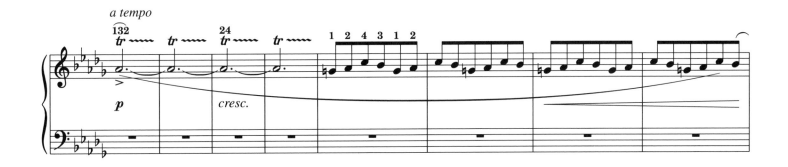

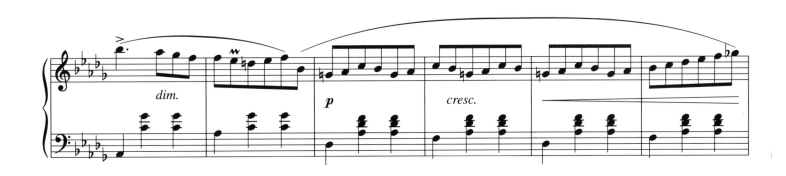

PRELUDE
(Op. 28, No. 20)

Frédéric Chopin

PRELUDE
(Op. 28, No. 6)

Frédéric Chopin

NOCTURNE
(Op. 9, No. 2)

Frédéric Chopin

PRELUDE
(Op. 28, No. 4)

Frédéric Chopin

CONSOLATION

Felix Mendelssohn

NOCTURNE
(Op. 55, No.1)

Frédéric Chopin

BERCEUSE

Charles Gounod

LOVE SONG

Adolf von Henselt

BERCEUSE

Halfdan Kjerulf

Andante

LA GONDOLA

Adolf von Henselt

MAZURKA
(Op. 7, No. 1)

Frédéric Chopin

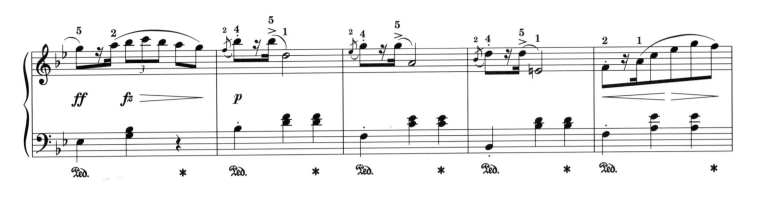

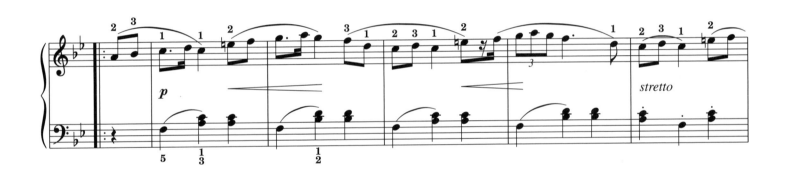

REMEMBRANCE
(Op. 68, No. 28)

Robert Schumann

Espressivo

TRÄUMEREI
(Op. 15, No. 7)

Robert Schumann

ROMANZE
(Op. 68, No. 19)

Robert Schumann

THE HAPPY FARMER

Robert Schumann

WHY?
(Op. 12, No. 3)

Robert Schumann

Lento e delicatamente

SPRING SONG

Felix Mendelssohn

WEDDING MARCH

(from *A Midsummer Night's Dream*)

Felix Mendelssohn

Allegro vivace

SLUMBER SONG
(Op. 124)

Robert Schumann

ritardando

a tempo

to Coda ⊕

EVENING SONG
(Op. 23, No. 4)

Robert Schumann

PETITE VALSE
(Op. 10, No. 2)

Genari Karganoff

AT SUNSET
(Op. 28, No. 5)

Edward MacDowell

Allegro con gajezza

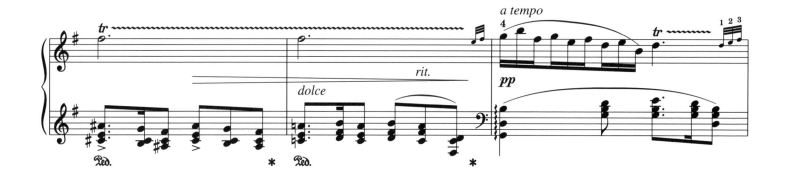

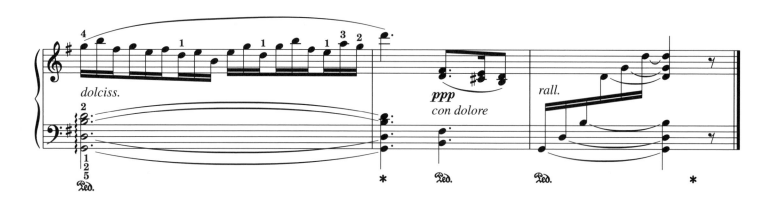

CANZONETTA

César Cui

CHANSON TRISTE
(Op. 40, No. 2)

Peter Ilyich Tchaikovsky

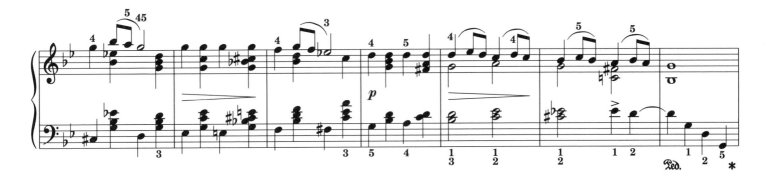

ROMANCE
(Op. 44, No. 1)

Anton Rubinstein

TOREADOR ET ANDALOUSE

Anton Rubinstein

CONSOLATION
(Op. 19, No. 6)

Theodore Leschetizky

Moderato *con espressione e ben legato la melodia*

EROTIK
(Op. 43, No. 5)

Edvard Grieg

SILHOUETTE

Antonín Dvořák

PAPILLON
(Butterfly)

Edvard Grieg

Allegro grazioso

ROMANCE

Adolf Jensen

MOMENT MUSICALE

Philipp Scharwenka

THE FLOW'RET
(Forest Idyl No. 1)

Edward MacDowell

ROMANCE
(Op. 2, No. 2)

Joseph Raff

Adagio quasi andante

CHANT SANS PAROLES

Peter Ilyich Tchaikovsky

Allegretto grazioso e cantabile

VALSE GRACIEUSE
(Op. 54, No. 1)

Antonín Dvořák

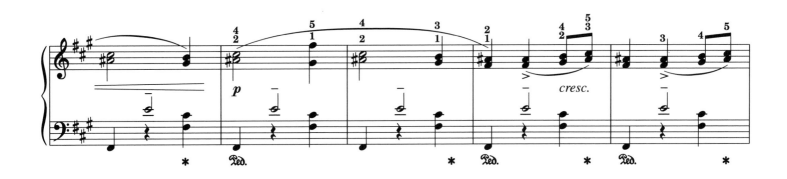

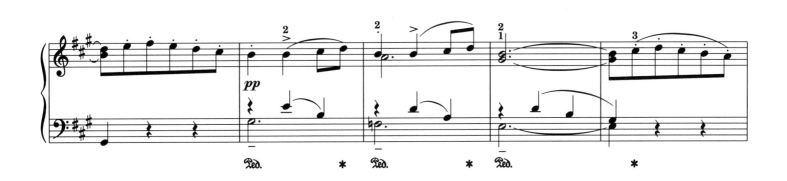

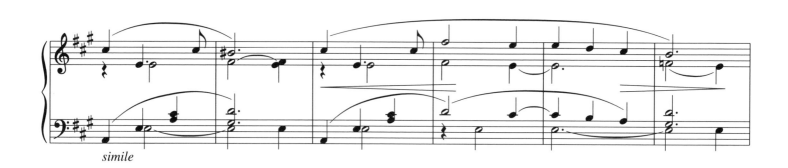

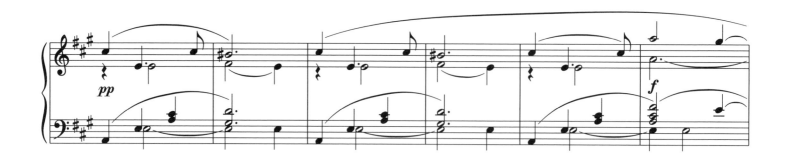

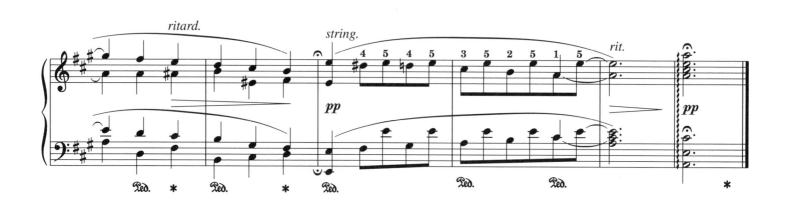

NOCTURNE
(from *Petite Suite*)

Alexander Borodin

174

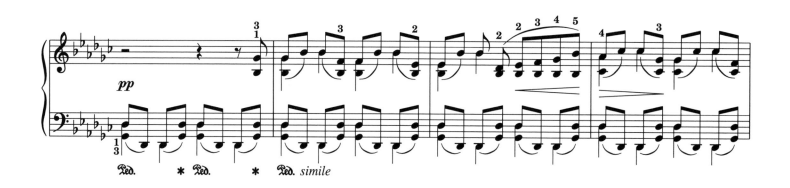

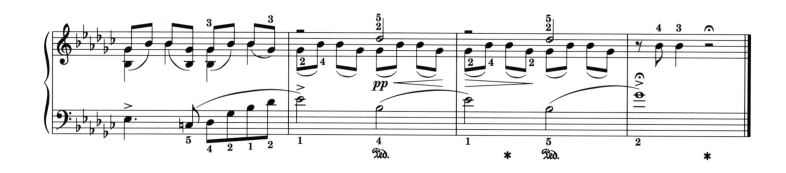

THE SWAN
(from *Carnival of the Animals*)

Camille Saint-Saëns

VILLANESCA
(Spanish Dance, Op. 5)

Enrique Granados

Andante espress.

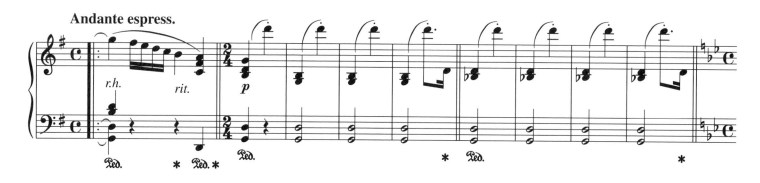

SONG & REFRAIN
Molto andante

HUMORESQUE
(Op. 101, No. 7)

Antonín Dvořák

Poco lento et gracioso

LIEBESTRÄUM
(Nocturne No. 3)

Poco allegro, con affetto

dolce cantando

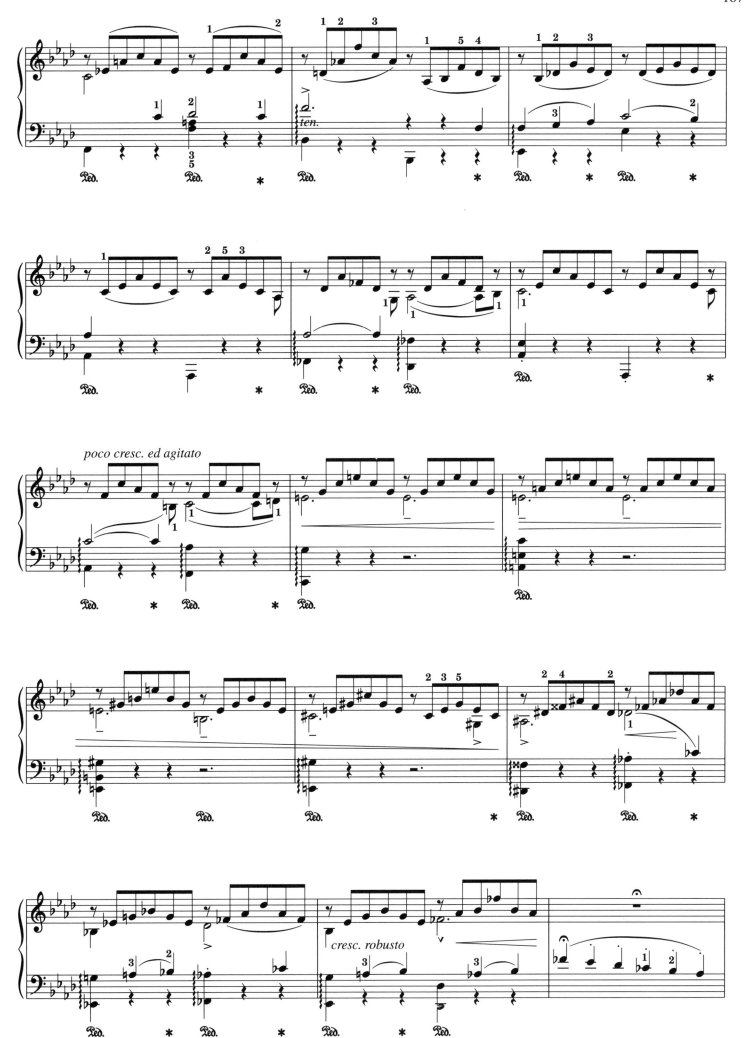

Più animato, con espressione

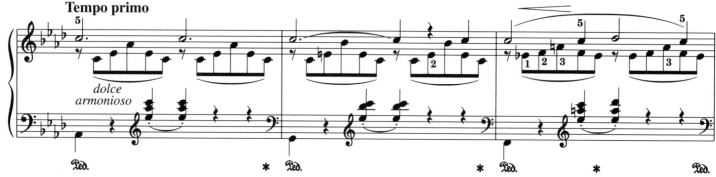

NORWEGIAN DANCE
(Op. 35, No. 2)

Edvard Grieg

ANITRA'S DANCE

(from *Peer Gynt*)

Edvard Grieg

MELODY IN F
(Op. 3, No. 1)

Anton Rubinstein

Moderato

ASE'S DEATH
(from *Peer Gynt*)

Edvard Grieg

Andante doloroso

ROMANCE
(Op. 5)

Peter Ilyich Tchaikovsky

BERCEUSE
(from *Jocelyn*)

Benjamin Godard

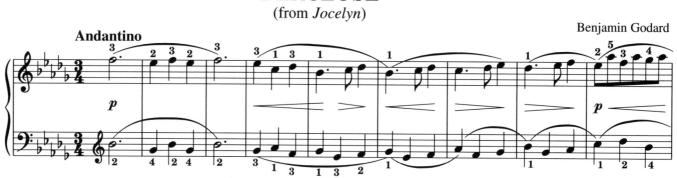

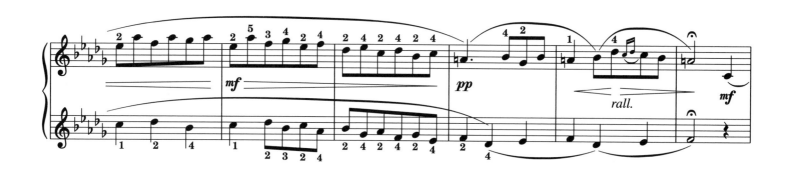

CONSOLATION NO.5

Franz Liszt

MAZURKA
(Op. 21, No. 1)

Camille Saint-Saëns

WALTZES
(Selected from Op. 39)

Johannes Brahms

Tempo giusto

SPRING DANCE

Edvard Grieg

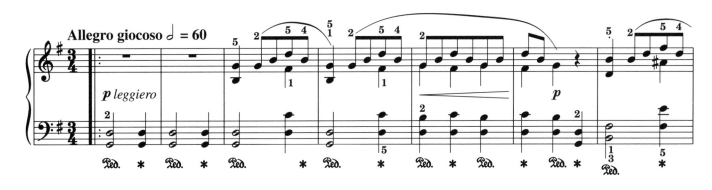

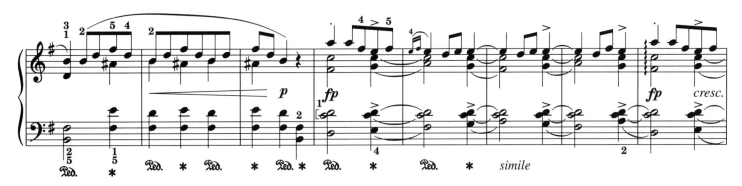

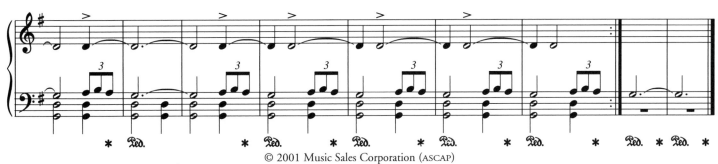

RÊVERIE

Claude Debussy

HUGARIAN DANCE NO. 5

Johannes Brahms

AU MATIN

Benjamin Godard

MELODIE
(Op. 10)

Jules Massenet

Lento, ma non troppo

ARABESKE

Genari Karganoff

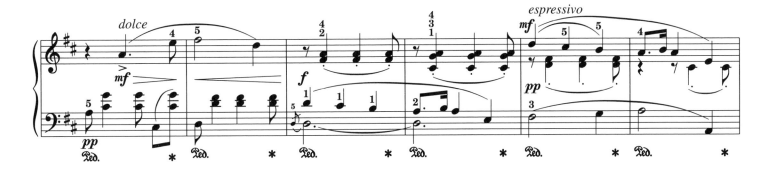

HABANERA

Emmanuel Chabrier

GOOD NIGHT

Albert Loeschhorn

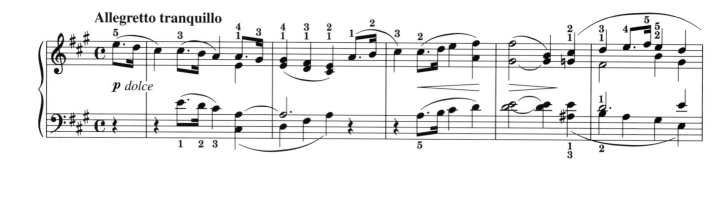

SIMPLE AVEU
(Simple Confession)

Francis Thomé

Moderato et legato

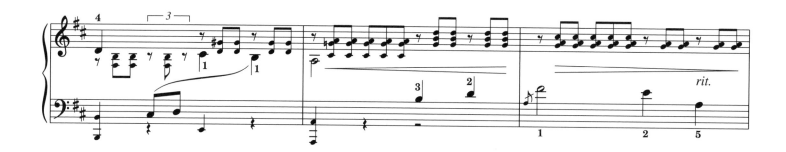

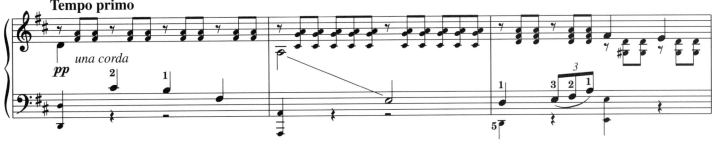

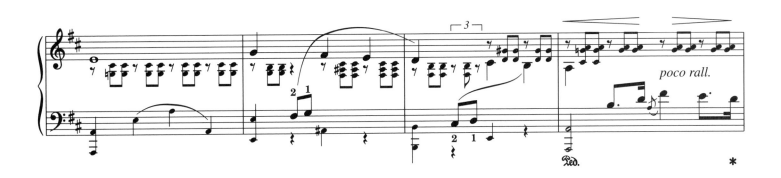

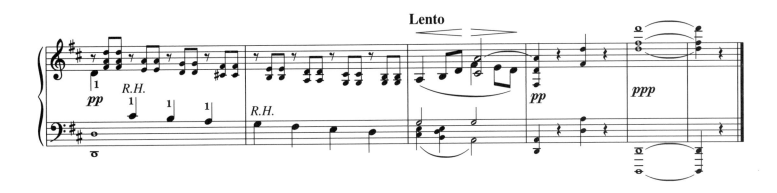

LOVE'S DREAM AFTER THE BALL
(Intermezzo)

Alphonse Czibulka

Returned from the ball, she falls asleep,
and in a charming vision, beholds him to
whom she has given her heart this night.

Andante amoroso
(The Vision)

ONE HEART, ONE MIND
(Polka Mazurka)

Johann Strauss

Fine

LONGING

Halfdan Kjerulf

LA PALOMA
(The Dove)

Sebastian Yradier

FLOWER SONG

Gustav Lange

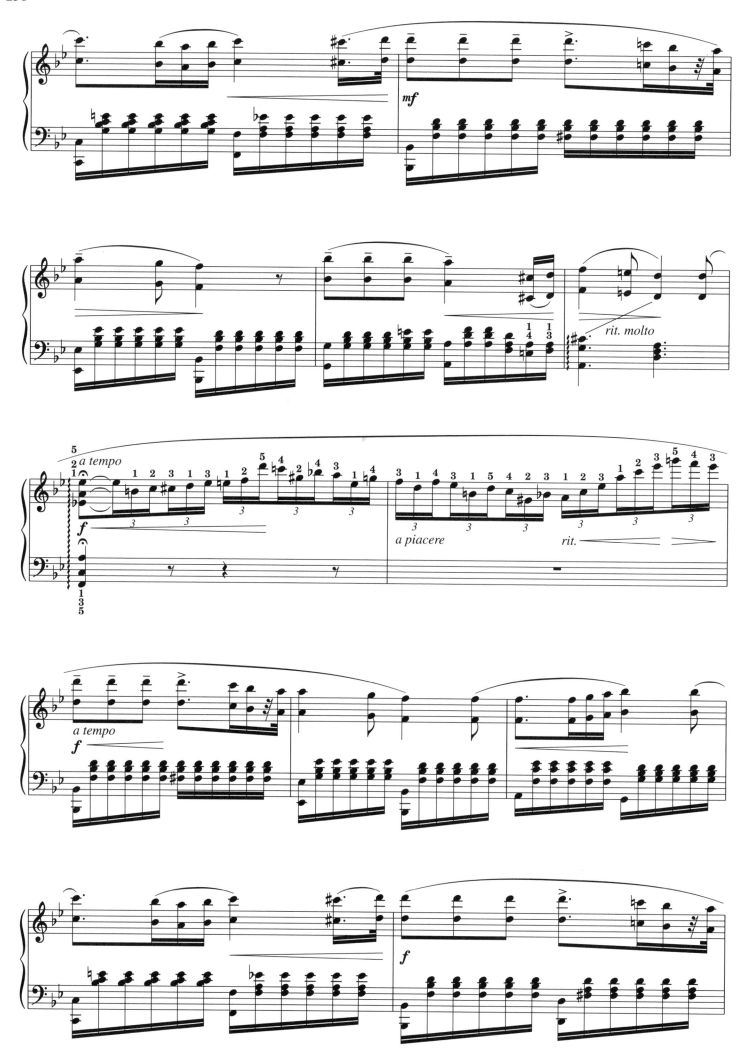

CRADLE SONG

Miska Hauser

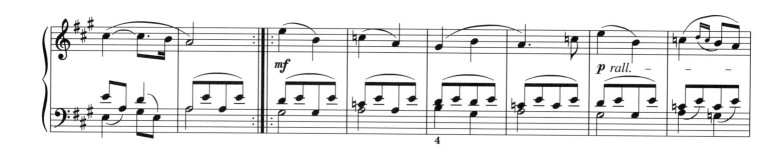

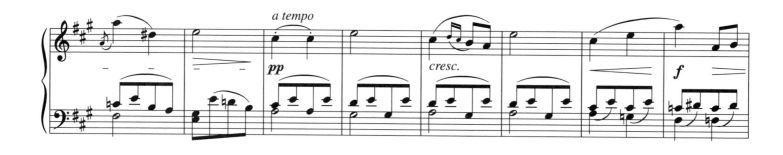

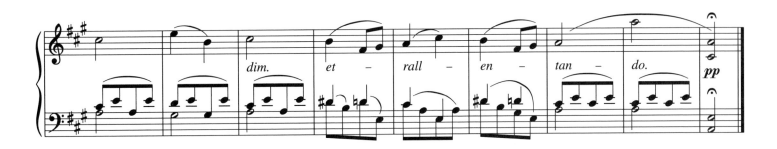

dim. *et – rall – en – tan – do.* **pp**

LE SECRET
(Intermezzo)

Leonard Gautier

Allegretto con moto

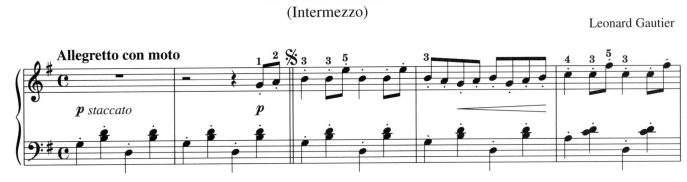

p staccato　*p*

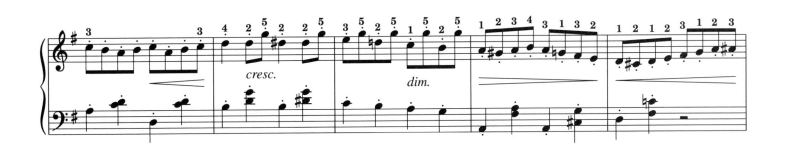

cresc.　*dim.*

p　*cresc.*

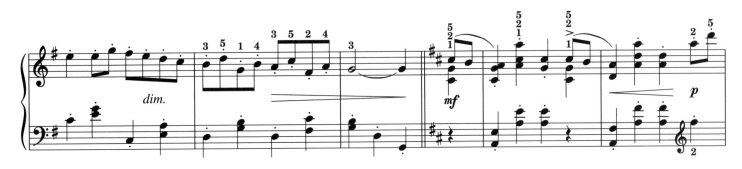

dim.　*mf*　*p*

D.S. al ⊕ to Coda

THE DYING POET
(Meditation)

Louis Moreau Gottschalk

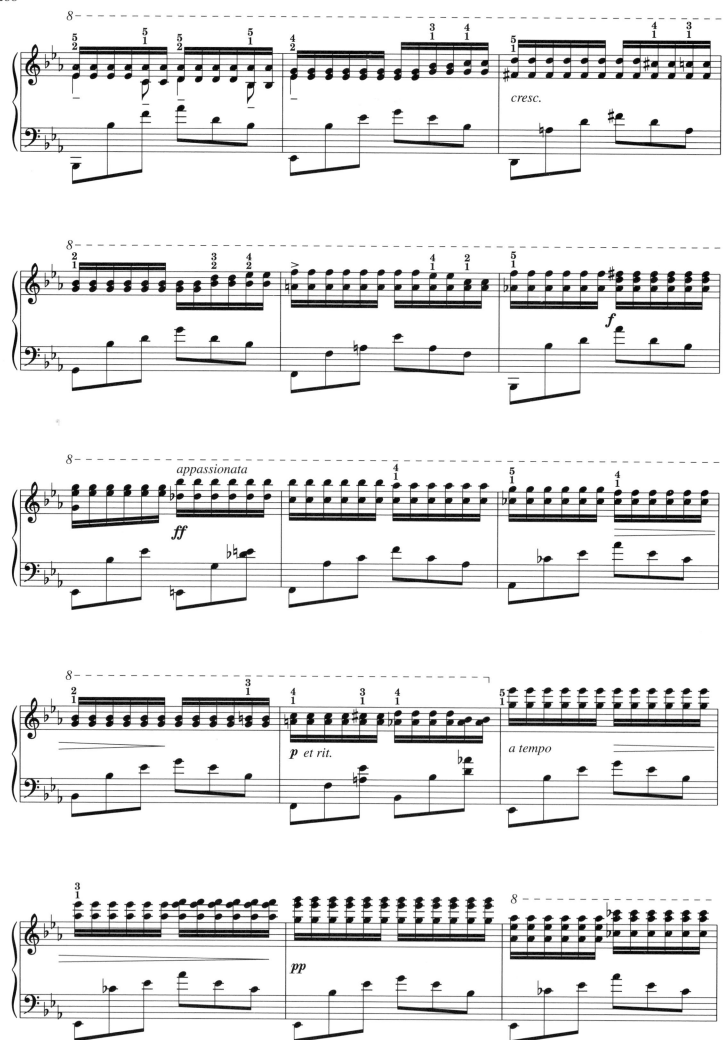

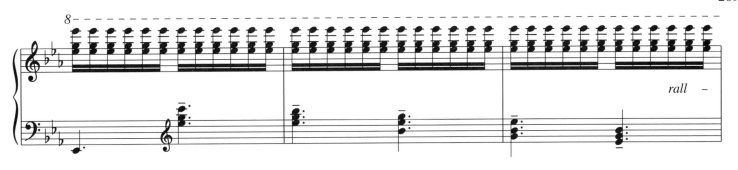

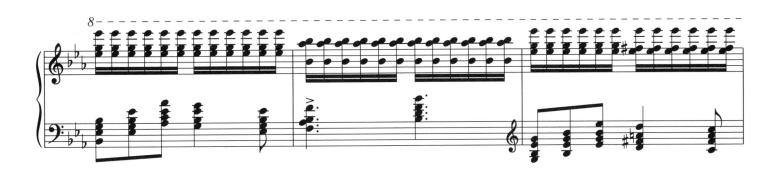

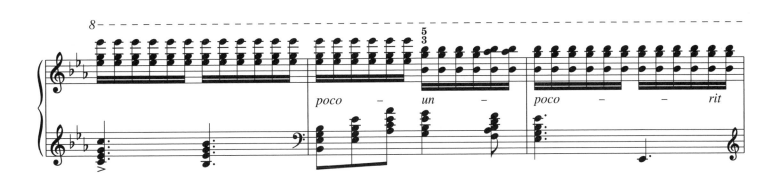

THINE OWN

Gustav Lange

PURE AS SNOW

Gustav Lange

THE SONG OF THE ROBIN

George William Warren

Allegretto pastorale

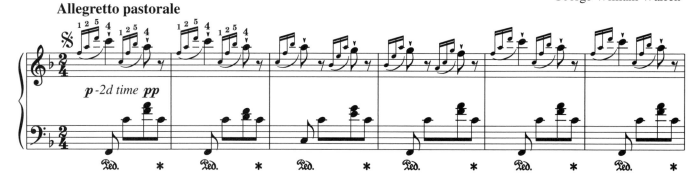

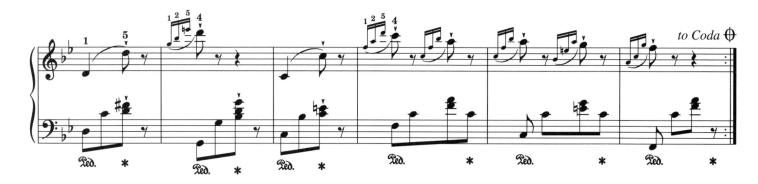

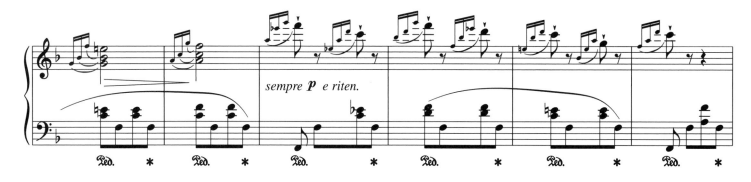

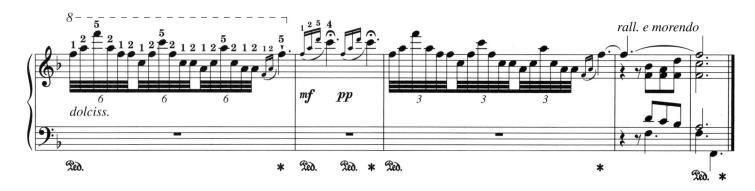

UNDER THE LEAVES
(Sous la feuilée)

Francis Thomé

THE LOST CHORD

Sir Arthur Sullivan

ADESTE FIDELES
(Paraphrase)

Renaud de Vilbac

LARGO
(from *Xerxes*)

George Frideric Handel

AVE MARIA

Franz Schubert

DEAD MARCH
(from *Saul*)

George Frideric Handel

INFLAMMATUS
(from *Stabat Mater*)

Gioacchino Rossini

Maestoso con moto

PLEYEL'S HYMN
(Transcription)

William Joseph Westbrook

HALLELUJAH CHORUS
(from *Messiah*)

George Frideric Handel

Allegretto moderato

BUT THE LORD IS MINDFUL

(from *St. Paul*)

Felix Mendelssohn

KOL NIDRE

Hebrew melody

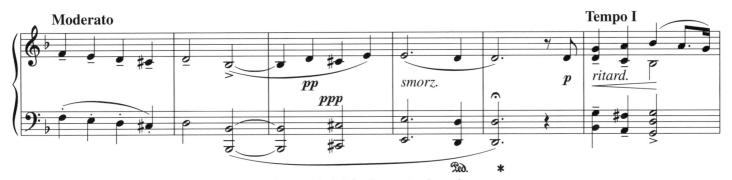

FUNERAL MARCH

(from *Sonata Op. 35*)

Frédéric Chopin

THE GLORY OF GOD IN NATURE

Ludwig van Beethoven

PRAYER
(Op. 48, No. 1)

Ludwig van Beethoven

THE HEAVENS ARE TELLING

(from *The Creation*)

AVE MARIA
(Meditation)

Johann Sebastian Bach & Charles Gounod

THE PALMS
(Les Rameaux)

Jean-Baptiste Fauré

SEXTETTE
(from *Lucia di Lammermoor*)

Gaetano Donizetti

Larghetto

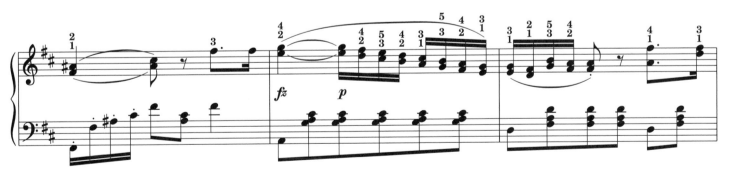

VALSE LENTE
(from *Coppelia*)

Léo Delibes

WALTZ
(from *Faust*)

Charles Gounod

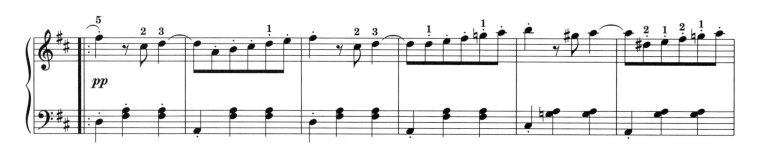

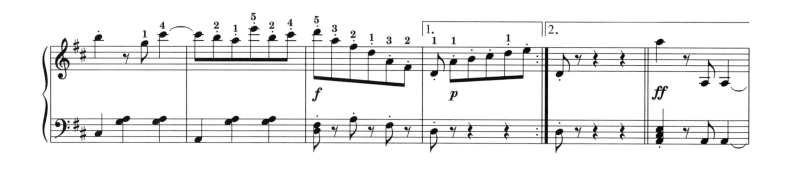

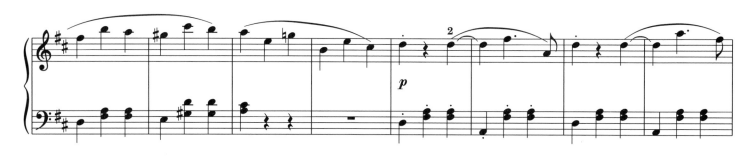

GRAND MARCH

(from *Aida*)

Giuseppe Verdi

MY HEART AT THY SWEET VOICE

(from *Samson and Delilah*)

Camille Saint-Saëns

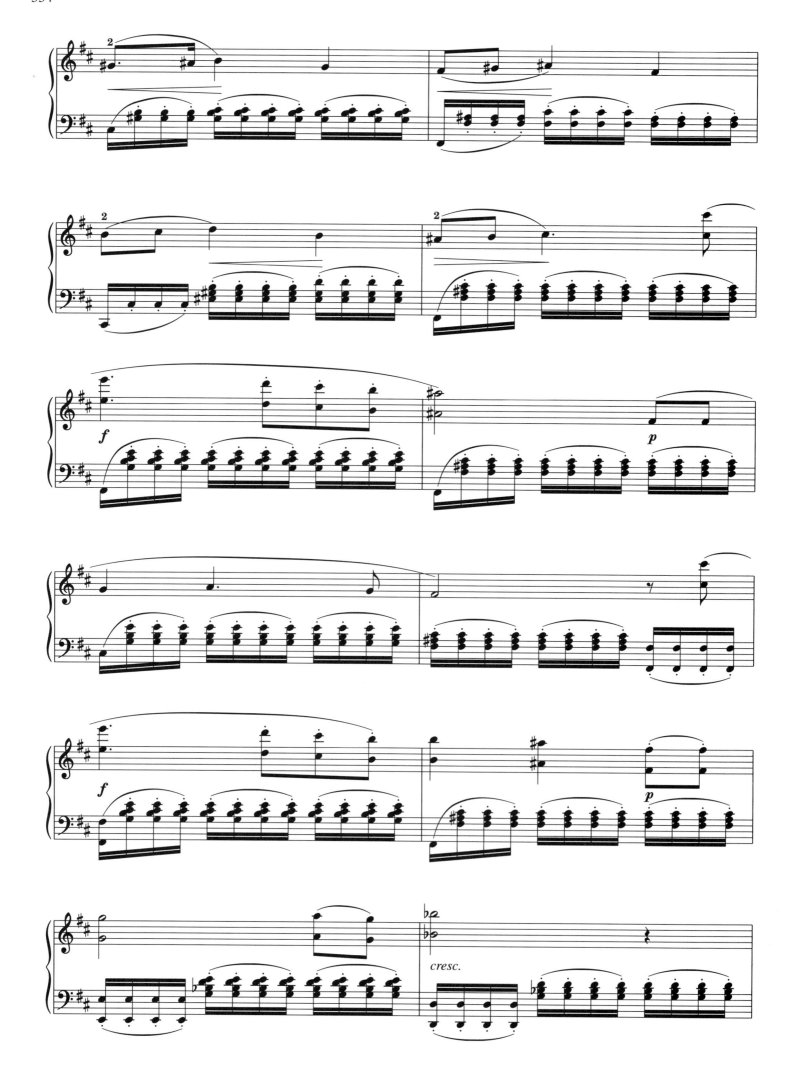

GRAND MARCH
(from *Norma*)

Vincenzo Bellini

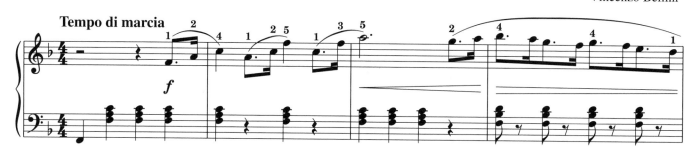

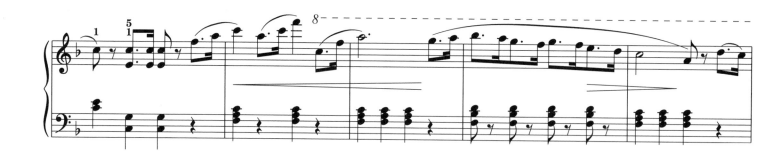

ARAGONAISE
(from *Le Cid*)

Jules Massenet

CORONATION MARCH

(from *Le Prophète*)

Giacomo Meyerbeer

Tempo di marcia molto maestoso

QUARTET
(from *Rigoletto*)

Giuseppe Verdi

MISERERE
(from *Il Trovatore*)

Giuseppe Verdi

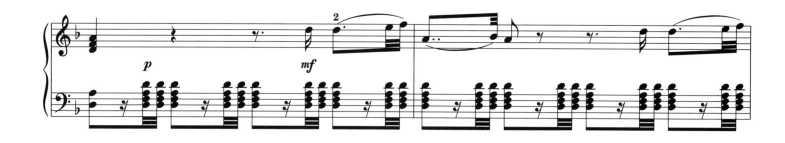

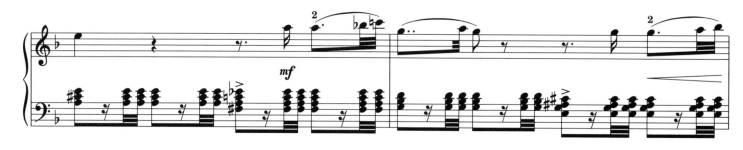

MINUET
(from *Don Juan*)

Wolfgang Amadeus Mozart

CELESTE AIDA
(from *Aida*)

Guiseppe Verdi

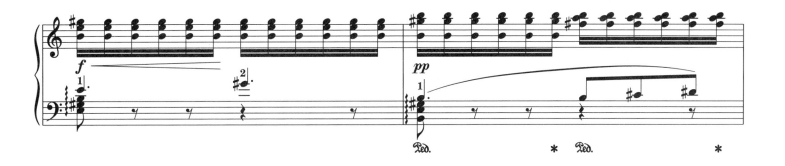

BRIDAL MARCH

(from *Lohengrin*)

Richard Wagner

TO THE EVENING STAR
(from *Tannhäuser*)

Richard Wagner

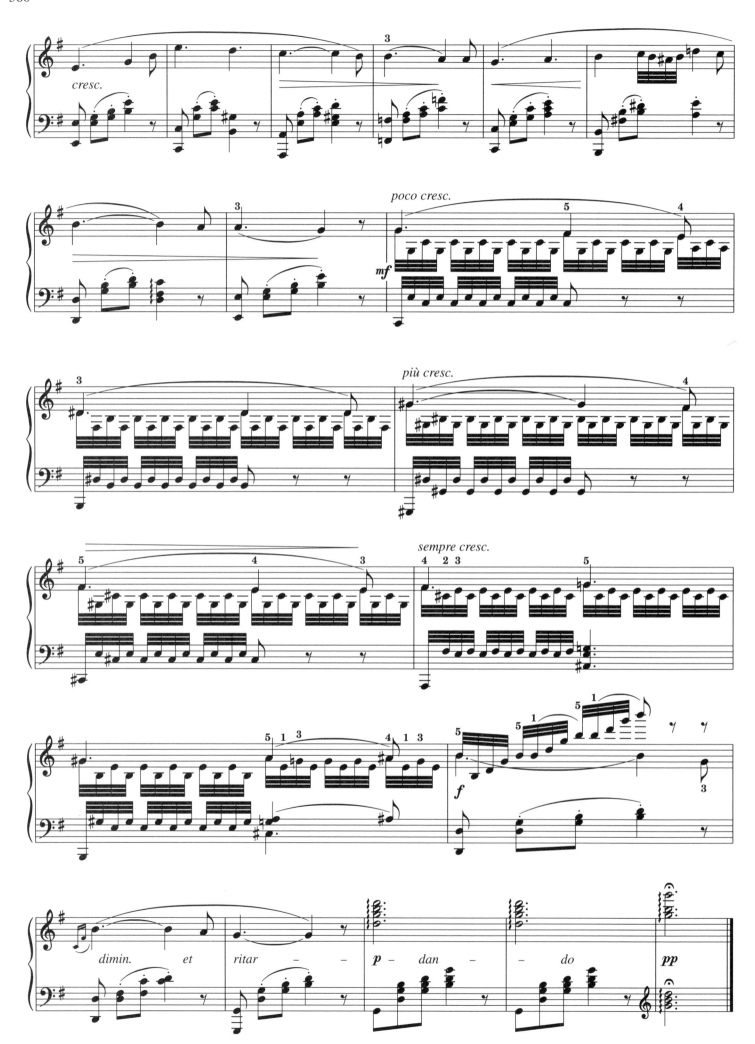

GRAND MARCH
(from *Tannhäuser*)

Richard Wagner

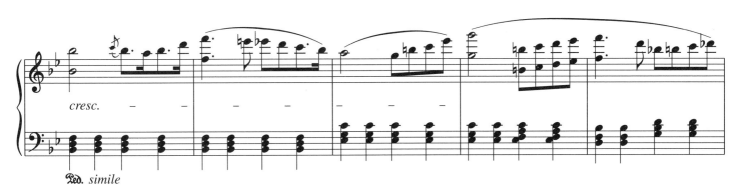

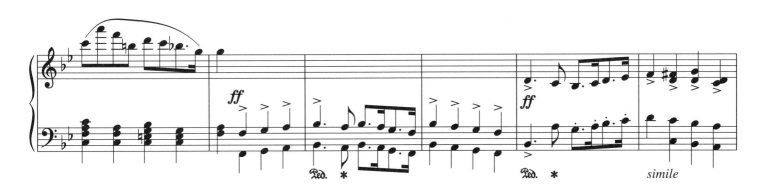

Maestoso (Overture)

WILLIAM TELL
(Excerpts)

Gioacchino Rossini

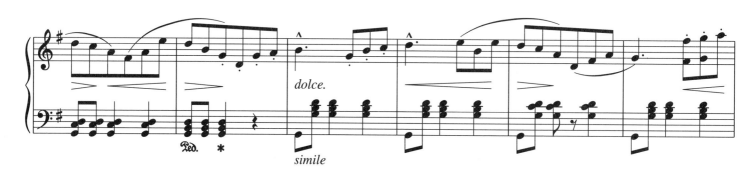

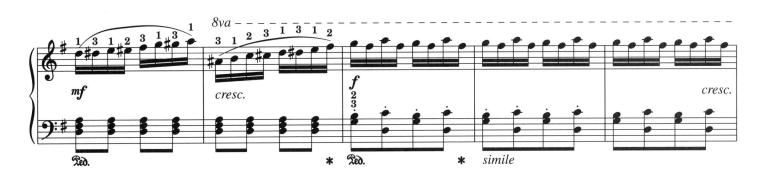

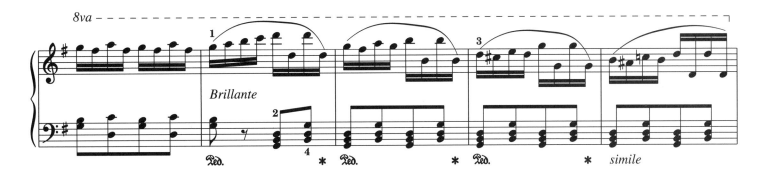

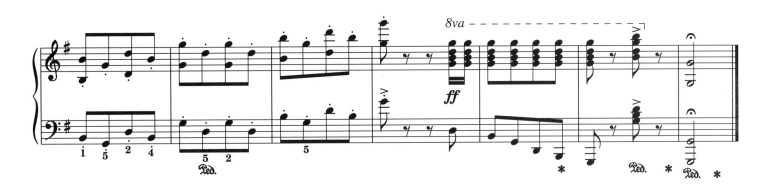

GAVOTTE
(from *Mignon*)

Ambroise Thomas

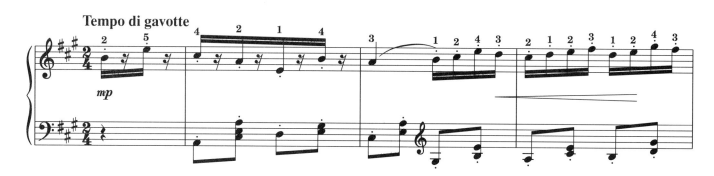

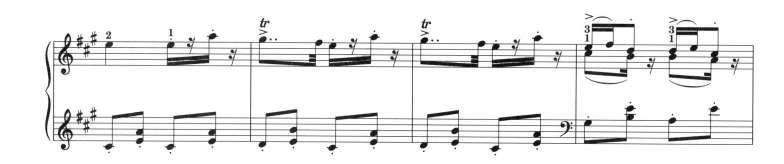

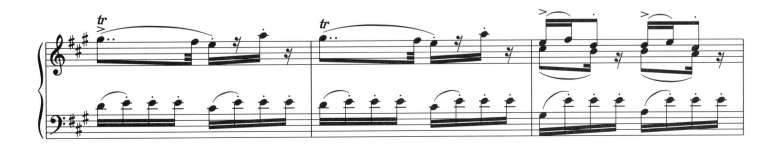

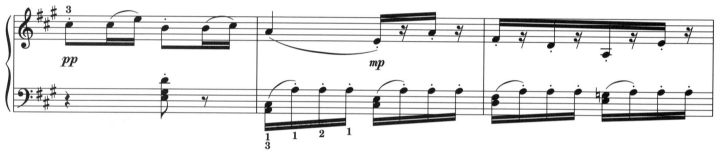

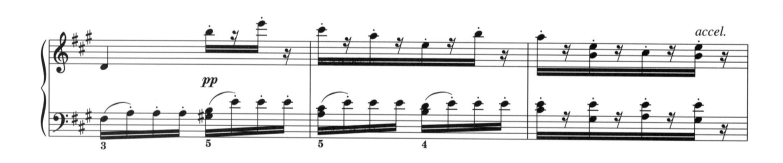

PIZZICATO
(from *Sylvia*)

Léo Delibes

HABANERA
(from *Carmen*)

Georges Bizet

ENTR'ACTE
(from *Rosamunde*)

Franz Schubert

DANCE OF THE HOURS

(from *La Gioconda*)

Amilcare Ponchielli

PRAYER

Carl Maria von Weber

BARCAROLLE
(from *Tales of Hoffman*)

Jacques Offenbach

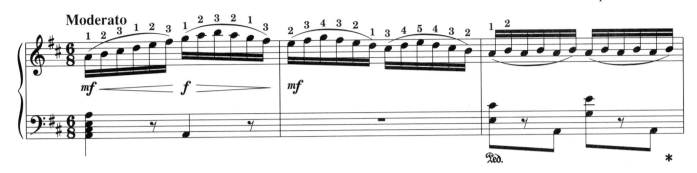

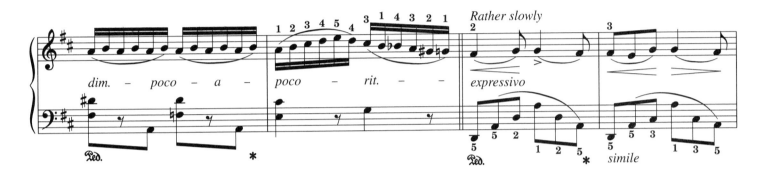

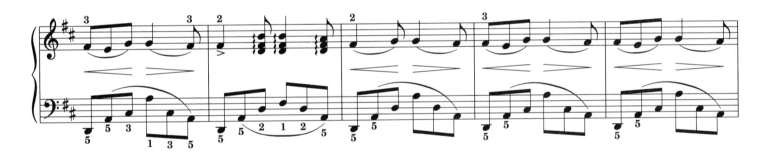

ANVIL CHORUS

(from *Il Trovatore*)

Giuseppe Verdi

PRAYER

(from *Hänsel and Gretel*)

Engelbert Humperdinck

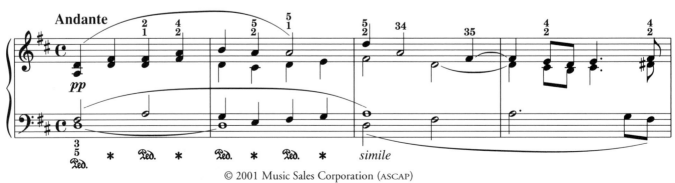

MARCH OF THE PRIESTS
(from *Athalie*)

Felix Mendelssohn

COMPOSER'S INDEX